REMBRANDT

MORTIMER MENPES

*WITH AN ESSAY ON THE LIFE AND WORK OF
THE ARTIST
BY C. LEWIS HIND*

ISBN: 1508971706
ISBN-13: 978-1508971702

Table of Contents

Paintings

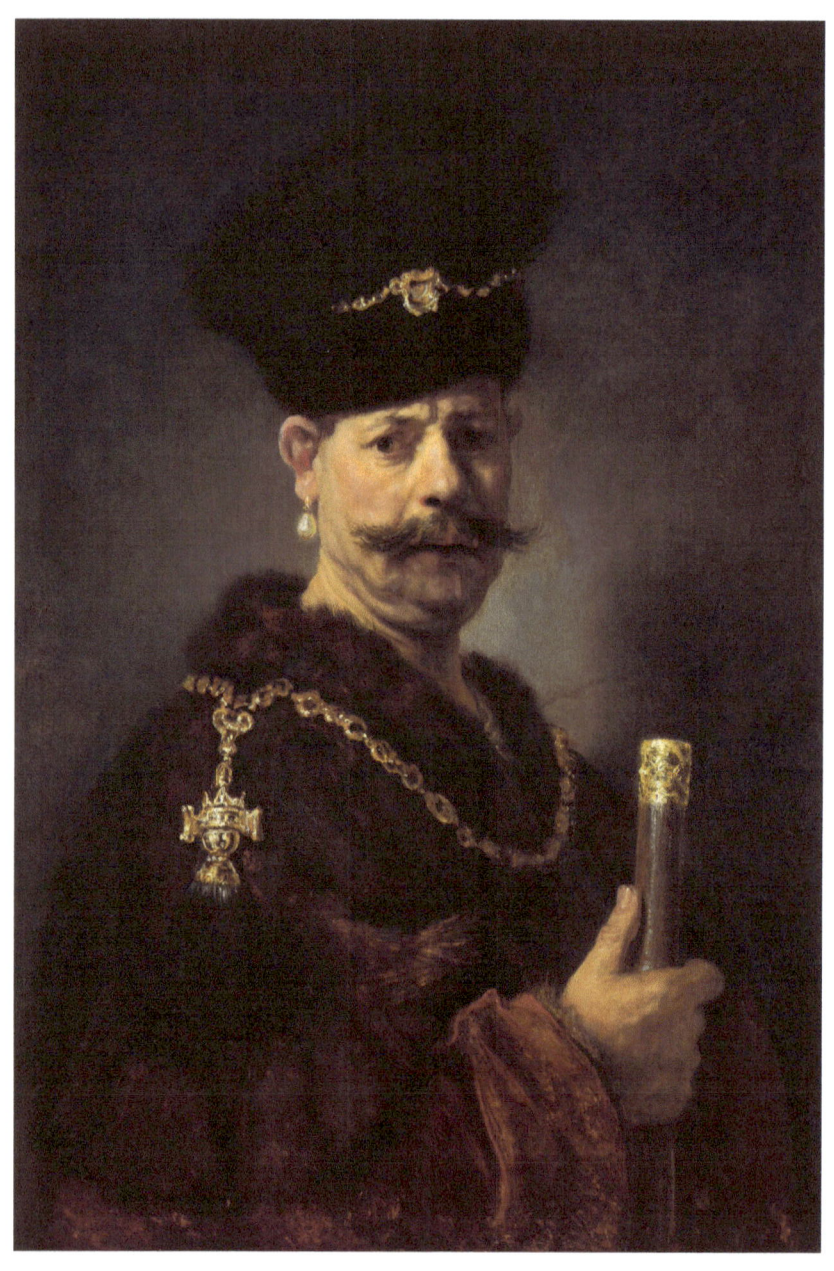

PORTRAIT OF A SLAV PRINCE 1637.
The Hermitage, St. Petersburg.

PREFACE

Although I am familiar with Rembrandt's work, through photographs and black and white reproductions, I invariably experience a shock from the colour standpoint whenever I come in touch with one of his pictures. I was especially struck with that masterpiece of his at the Hermitage, called the Slav Prince, which, by the way, I am convinced is a portrait of himself; any one who has had the idea suggested cannot doubt it for a moment; it is Rembrandt's own face without question. The reproductions I have seen of this picture, and, in fact, of all Rembrandt's works, are so poor and so unsatisfactory that I was determined, after my visit to St. Petersburg, to devise a means by which facsimile reproductions in colour of Rembrandt's pictures could be set before the public. The black and white reproductions and the photographs I put on one side at once, because of the impossibility of suggesting colour thereby.

Rembrandt has been reproduced in photograph and photogravure, and by every mechanical process imaginable, but all such reproductions are not only disappointing, but wrong. The light and shade have never been given their true value, and as for colour, it has scarcely been attempted.

After many years of careful thought and consideration as to the best, or the only possible, manner of giving to those who love the master a work which should really be a genuine reproduction of his pictures, I have adapted and developed the modern process of colour printing, so as to bring it into sympathy with the subject. For the first time these masterpieces, with all the rich, deep colouring, can be in the possession of every one—in the possession of the connoisseur, who knows and loves the originals but can scarcely ever see them, and in that of the novice, who hardly knows the emotions familiar to those who have made a study of the great masters, but is desirous of learning.

At the Hermitage in St. Petersburg I was specially privileged—I was allowed to study these priceless works with the glass off and in moments of bright sunlight—to see those sweeps of rich colour, so full, so clear, so transparent, and broken in places, allowing the undertones to show through.

I myself have made copies of a hundred Rembrandts in order to understand more completely his method of work. And in copying these pictures certain qualities have been revealed to me which no one could possibly have learnt except by this means. Rembrandt worked more or less in two stages: first, by a carefully-painted monochrome, handled in such a way as to give texture as well as drawing, and in which the masses of light and shade are defined in a masterly manner; second, by putting on the rich, golden colour—mostly in the form of glazes, but with a full brush. This method of handling glazes over monochrome has given a gem-like quality to Rembrandt's work, so much so that you might cut out any square inch from any portion of his pictures and wear it as a jewel. And in all his paintings there is the same decorative quality that I have before alluded to: any picture by Rembrandt arrests you as a decorative patch—the grouping and design, and, above all, the balance of light and shade, are perfect.

MORTIMER MENPES.

July 1905.

CHAPTER I.

THE RECOVERERS OF REMBRANDT

Imagine a man, a citizen of London, healthy, middle-aged, successful in business, whose interest in golf is as keen, according to his lights and limitations, as the absorption of Rembrandt in art. Suppose this citizen, having one day a loose half-hour of time to fill in the neighbourhood of South Kensington, remembers the articles he has skimmed in the papers about the Constantine Ionides bequest: suppose he strolls into the Museum and asks his way of a patient policeman to the Ionides collection. Suppose he stands before the revolving frame of Rembrandt etchings, idly pushing from right to left the varied creations of the master, would he be charmed? would his imagination be stirred? Perhaps so: perhaps not. Perhaps, being a man of importance in the city, knowing the markets, his eye-brows would unconsciously elevate themselves, and his lips shape into the position that produces the polite movement of astonishment, if some one whispered in his ear—"At the Holford sale the Hundred Guilder Print fetched £1750, and Ephraim Bonus with the Black Ring, £1950; and M. Edmund de Rothschild paid £1160 for a first state of the Dr. A. Tholinx." Those figures might stimulate his curiosity, but being, as I have said, a golfer, his interest in Rembrandt would certainly receive a quick impulse when he observed in the revolving frame the etching No. 683, 2-7/8 inches wide, 5-1/8 inches high, called The Sport of Kolef or Golf.

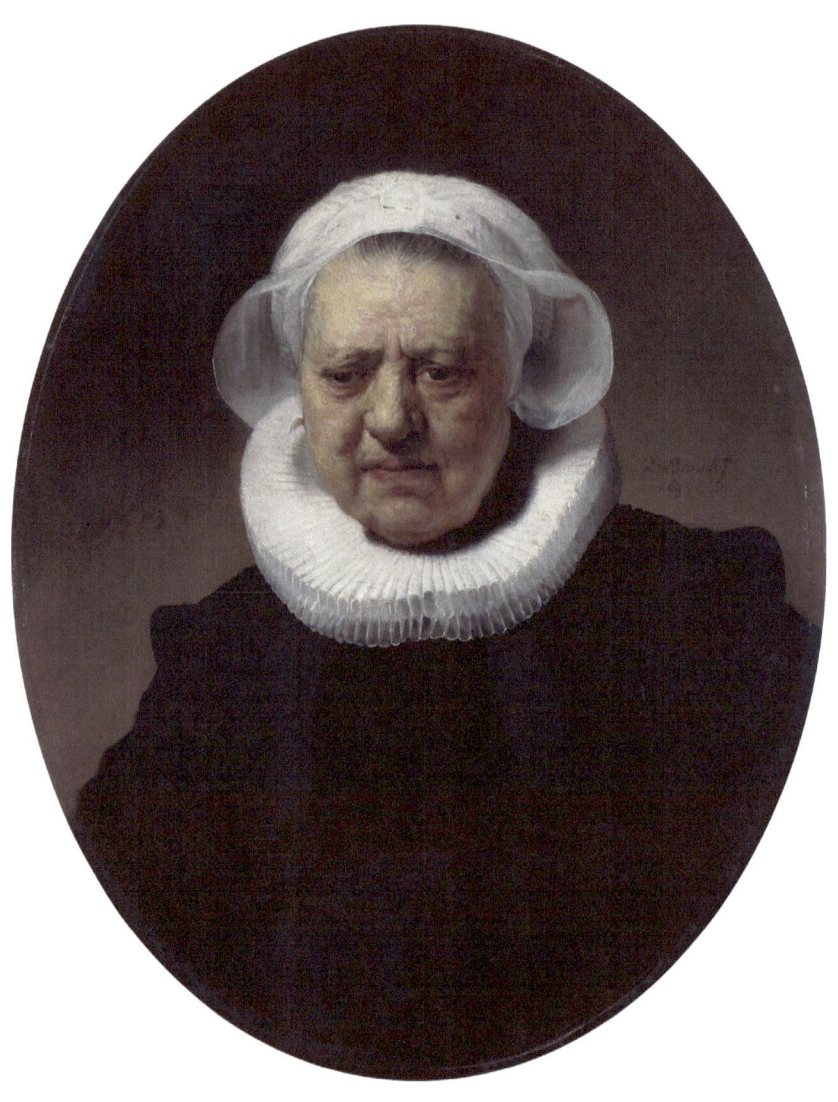

PORTRAIT OF A WOMAN OF EIGHTY-THREE

1634. National Gallery, London.

Is it fantastical to assume that his interest in Rembrandt dated from that little golf etching? Great events ofttimes spring from small causes. We will follow the Rembrandtish adventures of this citizen of London, and golfer. Suppose that on his homeward way from the Museum he stopped at a book shop and bought M. Auguste Bréal's small, accomplished book on Rembrandt. Having read it, and being a man of leisure, means, and grip, he naturally invested one guinea in the monumental tome of M. Émile Michel, Member of the Institute of France—that mine of learning about Rembrandt in which all modern writers on the master delve. Astonishment would be his companion while reading its packed pages, also while turning the leaves of L'Œuvre de Rembrandt, décrit et commenté, par M. Charles Blanc, de l'Academie Française. This sumptuous folio he picked up second hand and conveyed home in a cab, because it was too heavy to carry. Now he is fairly started on his journey through the Rembrandt country, and as he pursues his way, what is the emotion that dominates him? Amazement, I think.

Let me illustrate the extent and character of his amazement by describing a little incident that happened to him during a day's golfing at a seaside course on the following Saturday.

The approach to the sixteenth green is undeniably sporting. Across the course hangs the shoulder of a hill, and from the fastnesses of the hill a brook gushes down to the sea through the boulders that bestrew its banks. Obliged to wait until the preceding couple had holed out, our citizen and golfer amused himself by upturning one of the great lichen-stained boulders. He gazed into the dank pit thus disclosed to his eyes, and half drew back dismayed at the extraordinary activity of insect life that was revealed. It was so sudden, so unexpected. Beneath that grey and solemn boulder that Time and man accepted as a freehold tenant of the world, that our citizen had seen and passed a hundred times, a population of experts were working, their deeds unseen by the wayfarer. Now what is the meaning of this little story? How did the discovery of that horde of capable experts strike the imagination of our golfer? The boulder was Rembrandt. The busy insects were the learned and patient students working quietly on his behalf—his discoverers and recoverers. He had passed that boulder a hundred times, his eyes had rested cursorily upon it as often as the name of Rembrandt in book or newspaper had met his indifferent gaze. Now he had raised the boulder, as he had lifted the Rembrandt curtain, and lo! behind the curtain, as beneath the boulder, he had discovered life miraculously active.

Reverence for the students of art, for the specialists, for the scientific historians, was born within him as he pursued his studies in Rembrandt lore. Also he was conscious of sorrow, anger, and pride: sorrow for the artist of genius who goes down to his grave neglected, unwept, unhonoured, and unsung: anger at the stupidity and blindness of his contemporaries: pride at the unselfish industry and ceaseless activity of the men who, born years after, raise the master to his throne.

In the year 1669 an old Dutchman called Rembrandt dies in obscurity in Amsterdam. So unmemorable was the death deemed that no contemporary document makes mention of it. The passing of Rembrandt was simply noted, baldly and briefly, in the death-register of the Wester Kerk: "Tuesday, October 8, 1669; Rembrandt van Ryn, painter on the Roozegraft, opposite the Doolhof. Leaves two children." Yet once, while he was alive, before he painted The Night Watch, he had been the most famous painter in Holland. Later, oblivion encompassed the old lion, and little he cared so long as he could work at his art. Forty years after his death, Gerard de Lairesse, a popular painter, now forgotten, wrote

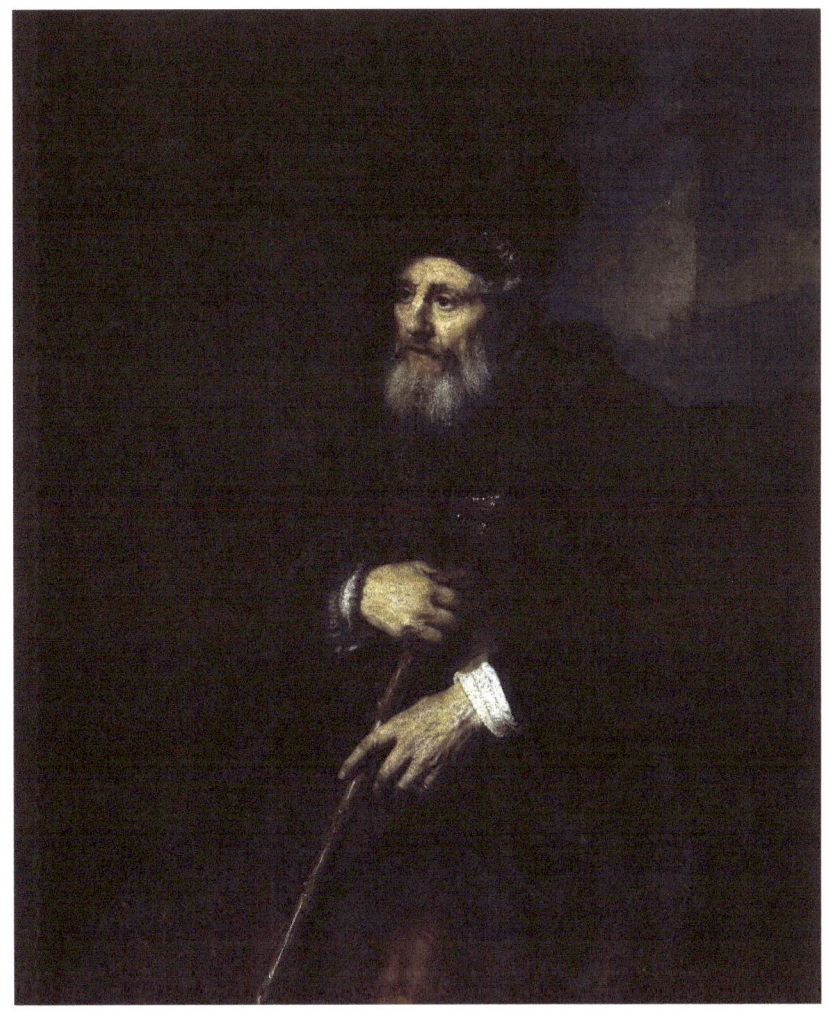

A RABBI SEATED, A STICK IN HIS HANDS AND A HIGH
FEATHER IN HIS CAP
1645. The Hermitage, St. Petersburg.

of Rembrandt—"In his efforts to attain a yellow manner, Rembrandt merely achieved an effect of rottenness.... The vulgar and prosaic aspects of a subject were the only ones he was capable of noting." Poor Gerard de Lairesse!

To-day not a turn or a twist of his life, not a facet of his temperament, not an individual of his family, friends, or acquaintances, not the slightest scrap of paper bearing the mark of his hand, but has been peered into, scrutinised, tracked to its source, and written about voluminously. The bibliography of Rembrandt would fill a library. Several lengthy and learned catalogues of his works have been published in volumes so large that a child could not lift one of them. His 450 pictures, his multitudinous drawings, his 270 etchings, their authenticity, their history, their dates, the identification of his models, have been the subjects of innumerable books and essays. Why, it would have taken our golfer three months just to read what has been written about one of Rembrandt's pictures—that known as The Night Watch. He might have begun with Bredius and Meyer of Holland, and M. Durand-Greville of France, and would then have been only at the beginning of his task. People make the long journey to St. Petersburg for the sake of the 35 pictures by Rembrandt that the Hermitage contains. He is hailed to-day as the greatest etcher the world has ever known, and there are some who place him at the head of that noble triumvirate who stand on the summit of the painters' Parnassus, Velasquez, Titian, and Rembrandt. Having browsed and battened on Rembrandt, and noted the countless cosmopolitan workers that for fifty years have been excavating the country marked on the art map Rembrandt, you can perhaps understand why our golfer likened the work of his commentators to the incessant activity that his upturning of that grey, lichen-covered boulder revealed.

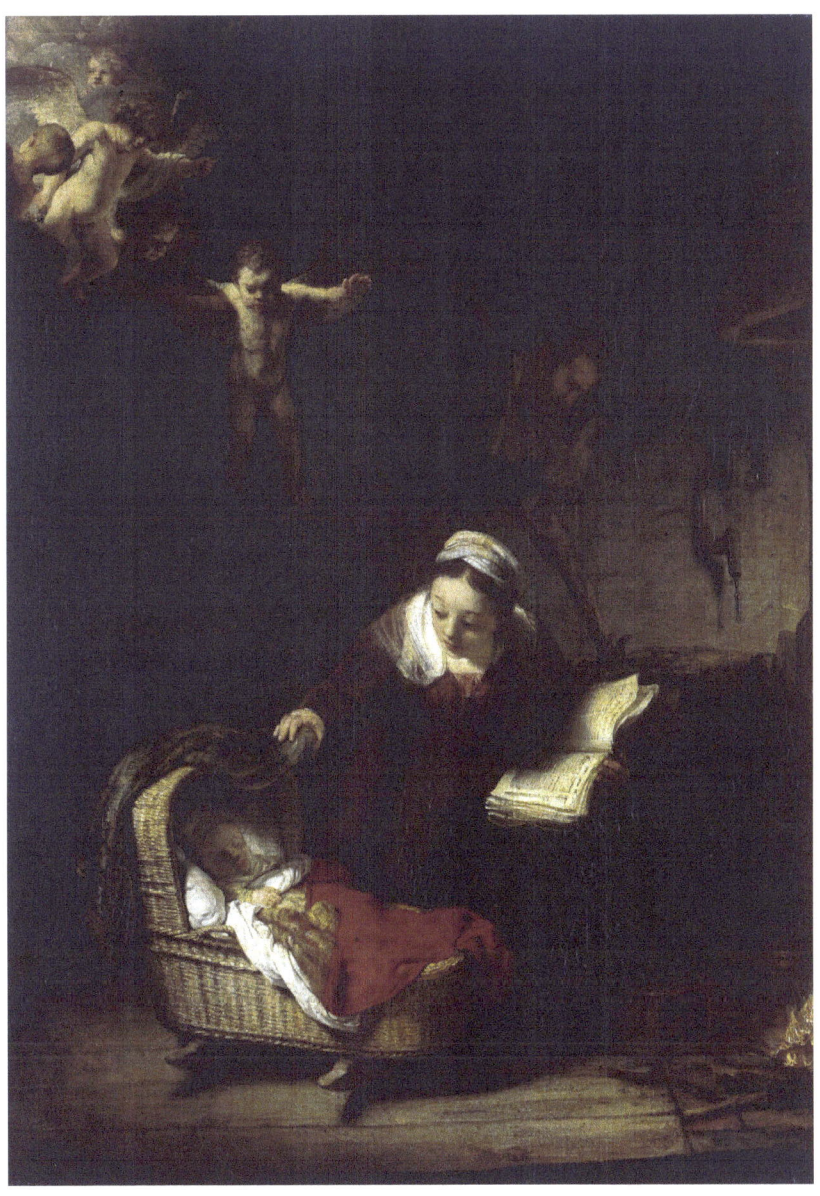

THE HOLY FAMILY WITH THE ANGELS

1645. The Hermitage, St. Petersburg.

But had our golfer, brimming with the modern passion for efficiency, learned foreign tongues, and browsed in the musty archives, he would have discovered that there was much to unlearn. The early scribes piled fancy upon invention, believing or pretending that Rembrandt was a miser, a profligate, a spendthrift, and so on. "Houbraken's facts," we read, "are interwoven with a mass of those suspicious anecdotes which adorn the plain tale of so many artistic biographies. Campo-Weyermann, Dargenville, Descamps, and others added further embellishments, boldly piling fable upon fable for the amusement of their readers, till legend gradually ousted truth."

All this and much more he would have had to unlearn, discovering in the end the simple truth that Rembrandt lived for his art; that he loved and was kind to his wife and to the servant girl who, when Saskia died, filled her place; that he was neither saint nor sinner; that he was extravagant because beautiful things cost money; that being an artist he did not manage his affairs with the wisdom of a man of the world; that he was hot-headed, and played a hot-headed man's part in the family quarrels; and that he was plucky and improvident, and probably untidy to the end, and that he did his best work when the buffets of fate were heaviest.

The new era in Rembrandt literature began with Kolloff's Rembrandt's Leben und Werke, published in 1854. This contribution to truth was followed by the works of Messrs. Bürger and Vosmaer, by the lucubrations of other meritorious bookworms, by the studies of Messrs. Bode and Bredius, and finally by M. Émile Michel's Life, which is the definitive and standard work on Rembrandt. Our golfer, whose French is a little rusty, was delighted to find when he gave the order for this book that it had been translated into English under the editorship of Mr. Frederick Wedmore. It was in the third edition.

He learned much from M. Émile Michel—among other things the herculean labour that is necessary if one desires to write a standard and definitive book on a subject. Not only did M. Michel visit and revisit all the galleries where Rembrandt's pictures are displayed in Russia, France, England, Sweden, Denmark, and North Germany, but he lived for several years with Rembrandt, surrounded by reproductions of his pictures, drawings, and etchings, and by documents bearing on their history, his mind all the while intently fixed on the facts of Rembrandt's life and the achievements of his genius. Gradually the procession of dates and facts took on a new significance; the heterogeneous threads of information wove themselves into the fabric of a life. M. Michel is the recoverer-in-chief of all that truly happened during the sixty-three years that Rembrandt passed upon this earth.

Every dead painter, poet, or writer of genius, has had his Recoverer. A searchlight has flashed upon all that Charles Lamb said, did, or wrote. Every forerunner who inspired Keats, from the day when he took the Faerie Queene like a fever, and went through it "as a young horse through a spring meadow, romping," has been considered and analysed. You could bury Keats and Lamb in the tomes that have been written about them. With the books of his commentators you could raise a mighty monument of paper and bindings to Rembrandt.

All this is very right and most worthy of regard. We do not sing "For they are jolly good fellows" in their honour, but we offer them our profound respect and gratitude. And our golfer, in his amateurish way, belongs to the tribe. He has approached Rembrandt through books. His temperament enjoyed exploring the library hive marked Rembrandt. Now he feels that he must study the works of the master, and while he is cogitating whether he shall first examine the 35 pictures at St. Petersburg, or the 20 in the Louvre, or the 20 at Cassel, or the 17 at Berlin, or the 16 at Dresden, or the 12 in the National Gallery, or the etchings and drawings in the print room of the British Museum, or the frame of etchings at South Kensington, so accessible, I drop him. Yes: drop him in favour of another who did not care two pins about the history or the politics of art, or the rights or wrongs of Rembrandt's life, but went straight to his pictures and etchings, wondered at them, and was filled with an incommunicable joy.

CHAPTER II.

THE APPEAL OF THE PAINTINGS

Suppose our citizen and golfer, deliberately dropped in the preceding chapter, had a child, a son, who by a freak of heredity was brooding and imaginative, fond, in a childish way, of pictures and books, but quite indifferent to scientific criticism and the methods of the analytic men. During his school holidays his mother would take him to the pantomime, and to the National Gallery. Dazed, he would scan the walls of pictures, wondering why so many of them dealt with Scriptural subjects, and why some were so coloured, and others so dim.

But after the third or fourth visit this child began to recognise favourites among the pictures, and being somewhat melancholy and mystical by nature, liking trees, beechwood glades, cathedral aisles, and the end of day, he would drag upon his mother's arm when they passed two pictures hanging together in the Dutch room. One was called The Woman taken in Adultery, the other, The Adoration of the Shepherds. These pictures by Rembrandt attracted him: they were so different from anything else in the gallery. He did not trouble to understand their meaning; he did not dwell upon the beauty of the still figure of Christ, or note that the illumination in The Adoration of the Shepherds proceeded from the supernatural light that shines from the Infant Jesus. What captivated him was the vastness contained in these small pictures, and the eerie way in

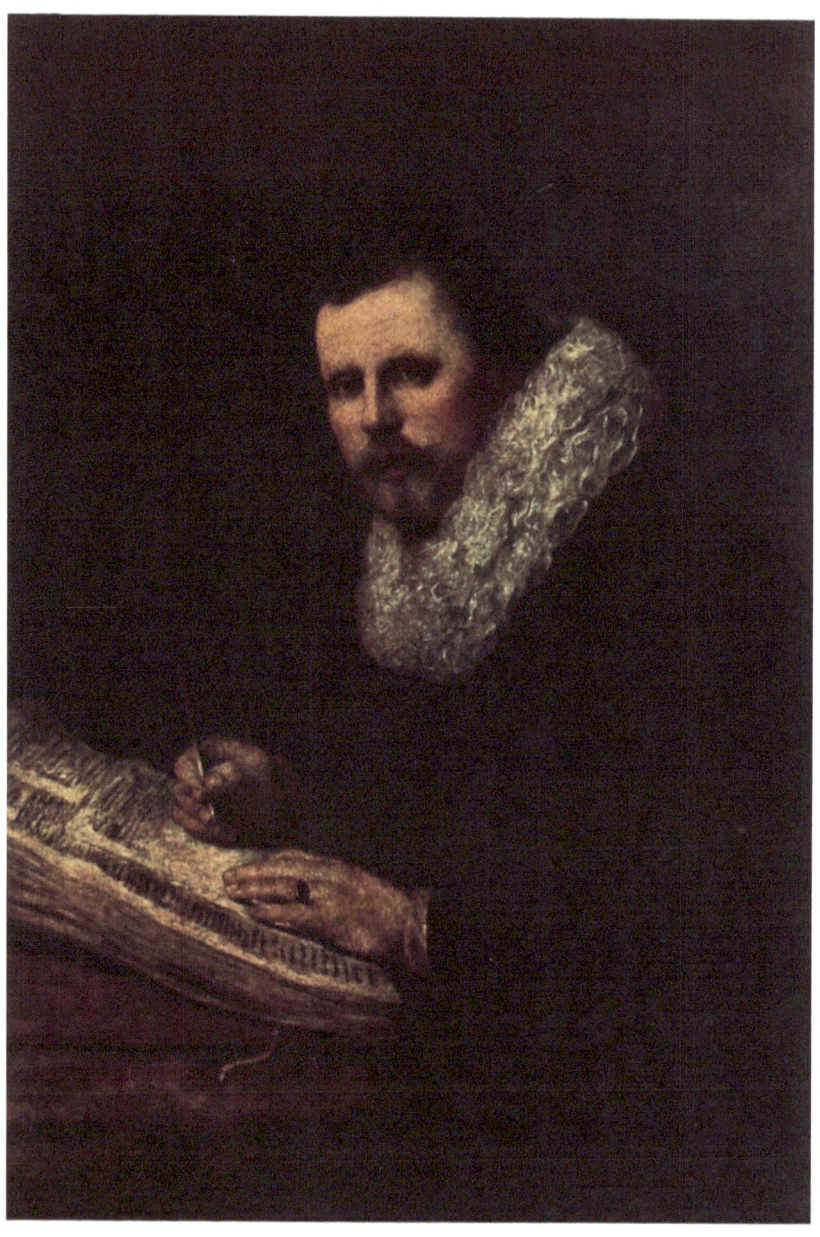

PORTRAIT OF A SAVANT

1631. The Hermitage, St. Petersburg.

which the light was separated from the dark. He had never seen anything like it before, but these pictures made him long to be grown up and able to seek such sights. He could see the lurking shadows alone in his bed at night, and held his breath when he thought of the great darkness that stretched out to the frames of the pictures. He wondered if temples were really as mysterious and dim as the great building that loomed above the small dazzling figure of the kneeling penitent and that horrid man who, his mother told him, was one of her accusers.

When she came into his bedroom to see that he was safely tucked up for the night, this child asked his mother why Rembrandt's pictures were so different from the pictures of other painters.

She explained that Rembrandt was a great master of chiaroscuro, making a valiant attempt to pronounce the uncomfortable word.

"What does that mean?" asked the little boy.

"It—er—means—One moment, dear; I think I hear your father calling."

She ran downstairs and consulted the dictionary.

"A chiaroscurist," she told her little boy when she returned to the bedroom, "is a painter who cares for and studies light and shade rather than colour. Now go to sleep. You're too young to bother about such things."

This child's mother was an ardent Ruskinian. Observing that her husband, the citizen and golfer, was asleep in his chair when she returned from her son's bedroom, she stepped into the library, picked Modern Painters from the shelf, and read the following passages, gravely shaking her head occasionally as she read.

"... Rembrandt always chooses to represent the exact force with which the light on the most illumined part of an object is opposed to its obscurer portions. In order to obtain this, in most cases, not very important truth, he sacrifices the light and colour of five-sixths of his picture; and the expression of every character of objects which depends on tenderness of shape or tint. But he obtains his single truth, and what picturesque and forcible expression is dependent upon it, with magnificent skill and subtlety.

"... His love of darkness led also to a loss of the spiritual element, and was itself the reflection of a sombre mind....

"... I cannot feel it an entirely glorious speciality to be distinguished, as Rembrandt was, from other great painters, chiefly by the liveliness of his darkness and the dulness of his light. Glorious or inglorious, the speciality itself is easily and accurately definable. It is the aim of the best painters to paint the noblest things they can see by sunlight. It was the aim of Rembrandt to paint the foulest things he could see—by rushlight...."

Had Ruskin, one wonders, ever seen The Syndics at Amsterdam, or the Portrait of his Mother, and the Singing Boy at Vienna, or The Old Woman at St. Petersburg, or the Christ at Emmaus at the Louvre, or any of the etchings?

The time came when the child was allowed to visit the National Gallery unattended; but although he never lost his affectionate awe for the two dim interiors, he did not really begin to appreciate Rembrandt until he had reached manhood. Rembrandt is too learned in the pathos of life, too deeply versed in realities, to win the suffrages of youth. But he was attracted by another portrait in the National Gallery—that called A Jewish Rabbi. This was the first likeness he had seen of a Rabbi, a personality dimly familiar to him through the lessons in church and his school Scripture class. Remembering what his mother had told him about chiaroscuro, he noted how the golden-brown light is centred upon the lower part of the face; how the forehead is in shadow, and how stealthily the black hat and coat creep out from the dark background. He had never seen, and never could have imagined, such a sad face. This Rabbi seemed to be crouching into the picture as he dimly understood that Jews in all ages, except those who owned diamond mines in South Africa, had cringed under the hand of their oppressors.

He wondered how Rembrandt knew what a Rabbi was like. His father might have told him that Rembrandt's pencil and brush were never idle, that he was for ever making pictures of himself, of his father, of his mother, of his wife, of his children and relations, of every interesting type that came within the ken of his piercing eyes; that one day, when he was prowling about the Jews' quarter at Amsterdam, he saw an old, tired, wistful Hebrew sitting in the door of his shop, engaged him in conversation, persuaded him to sit for his portrait, and lo! the nameless Amsterdam Jew became immortal.

His father might also have told him (perhaps he did) that the artist, wherever he goes, sometimes hardly aware of his preoccupation, is always selecting subjects to paint, and brooding over the method of treatment; that one day Rembrandt noted with amusement a man in the street shaking his fist at the skull-capped head of an older man bobbing angrily from a window. Rembrandt chuckled, remembered the incident, painted it, and called it, for a picture must have a title, Samson threatening his Father-in-law; that one day Rembrandt saw a fair-haired, chubby boy learning his lessons at his mother's knee. The composition appealed to his artist eye, he painted it, and the result is that beautiful and touching picture in the Hermitage Gallery at St. Petersburg called Hannah teaching Samuel his Lessons.

To a child, the portrait of a painter by himself has a human interest apart altogether from its claim to be a work of art. Rembrandt's portrait of himself at the National Gallery, painted when he was thirty-two, is not one of his remarkable achievements. It is a little timid in the handling, but that it is an excellent likeness none can doubt. This bold-eyed, quietly observant, jolly-looking man was not quite the presentment of Rembrandt

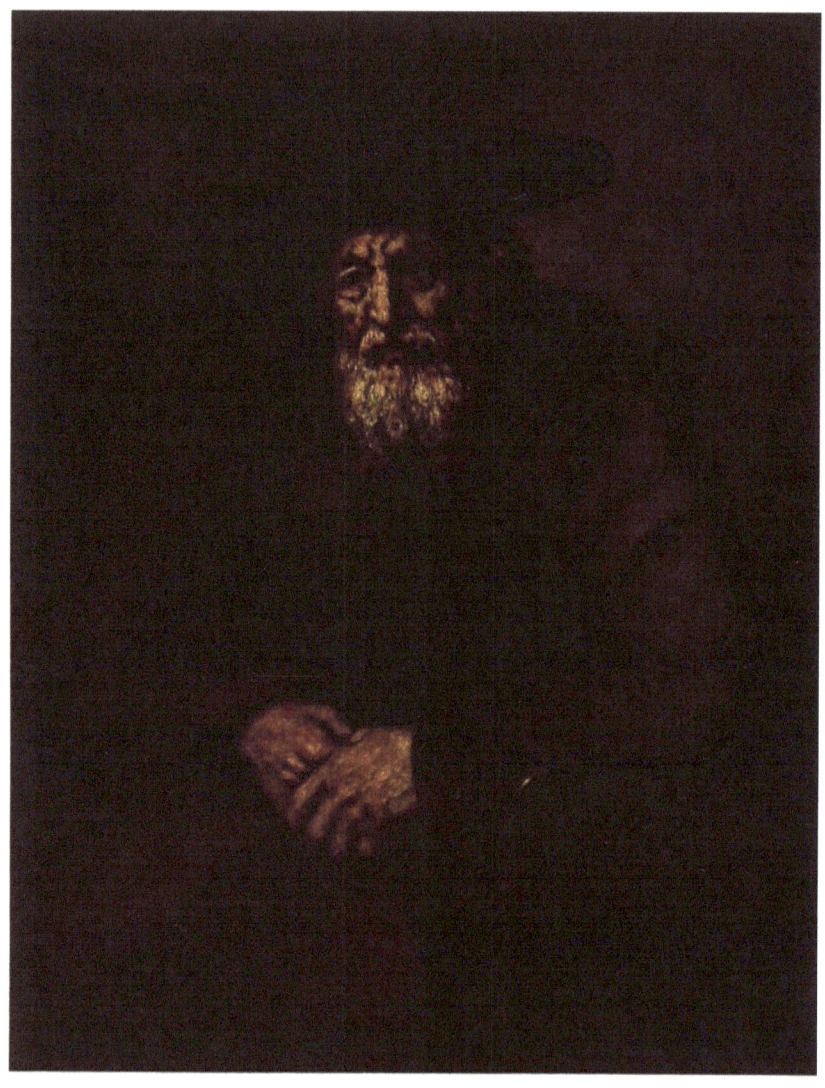

AN OLD MAN WITH A LONG WHITE BEARD, SEATED,
WEARING A WIDE CAP, HIS HANDS FOLDED
1654. The Hermitage, St. Petersburg.

that the child had imagined; but Rembrandt at this period was something of a sumptuous dandy, proud of his brave looks and his fur-trimmed mantle. Life was his province. No subject was vulgar to him so long as it presented problems of light and construction and drawing. Rembrandt, like Montaigne, was never didactic. He looked at life through his eyes and through his imagination, and related his adventures. One day it was a flayed ox hanging outside a butcher's shop, which he saw through his eyes; another day it was Christ healing the sick, which he saw through his imagination. You can imagine the healthy, full-blooded Rembrandt of this portrait painting the Carcase of a Bullock at the Louvre, or that prank called The Rape of Ganymede, or that delightful, laughing picture of his wife sitting upon his knee at Dresden, which Ruskin disliked.

The other portrait of Rembrandt by himself at the National Gallery shows that he was not a vain man, and that he was just as honest with himself as with his other sitters. It was painted when he was old and ailing and time-marked, five years before his death. His hands are clasped, and he seems to be saying—"Look at me! That is what I am like now, an old, much bothered man, bankrupt, without a home, but happy enough so long as I have some sort of a roof above me under which I can paint. I am he of whom it was said that he was famous when he was beardless. Observe me now! What care I so that I can still see the world and the men and women about me—'When I want rest for my mind, it is not honours I crave, but liberty.'"

Twenty-eight seemed a great age to the child; but he thought it wonderful that the portrait of an Old Lady at the National Gallery should have been painted when Rembrandt was but twenty-eight. She was too strong and determined for his liking, and he wondered why some of Rembrandt's pictures, like The Woman taken in Adultery, should be so mysterious and poetical, and others like this old lady so lifelike and straightforward.

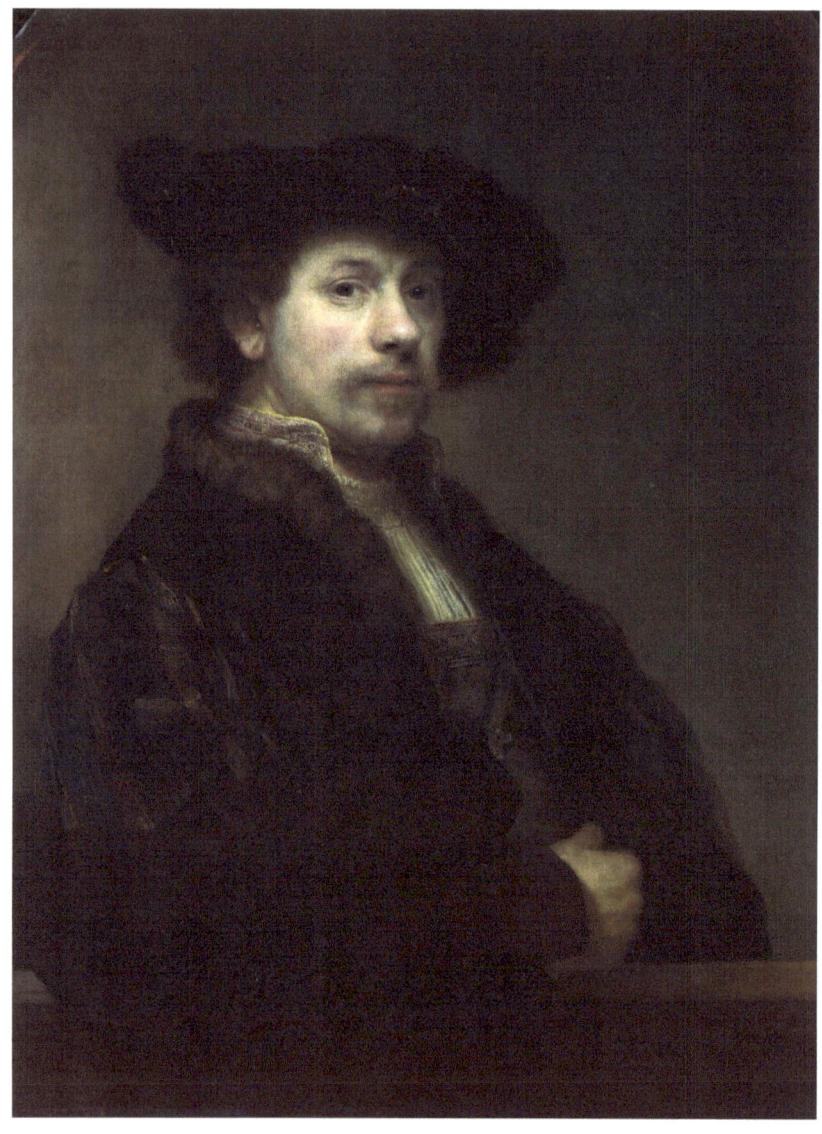

REMBRANDT LEANING ON A STONE SILL
1640. National Gallery, London.

He was too young to understand that the composition of the fortuitous concourse of atoms called Rembrandt, included not only the power that Velasquez possessed in so supreme a degree of painting just what his eyes saw, exemplified by this portrait of An Old Lady, aged 83, and by the portrait of Elizabeth Bas at Amsterdam, but that it also included the great gift of creative imagination, exemplified by the Christ at Emmaus, and The Good Samaritan of the Louvre, and in a way by the Portrait of a Slav Prince at the Hermitage, where a man in the alembic of Rembrandt's imagination has become a type. Also in The Reconciliation of David and Absalom at the Hermitage, where behind the sham trappings of the figures shine the eternal motives of reconciliation and forgiveness.

When the child was much older he saw the Christ at Emmaus, and The Good Samaritan in the little room at the Louvre, hanging side by side, and he never forget the hour that he spent with them. He had seen, year by year, many of the world's pictures; but at the sight of these two works, his childish predilection for Rembrandt became a deep-rooted reverence and admiration, which was never to pass from him.

Here was Rembrandt the seer, the man who had suffered. Saskia was dead, his popularity gone; but the effect of these things was but to fill his heart with a world sympathy, with pity for all who sorrow. Again and again he treated the Christ at Emmaus, The Good Samaritan, and The Prodigal Son themes. "Some strange presentment of his own fate," says M. Michel, "seems to have haunted the artist, making him keenly susceptible to the story of The Good Samaritan. He too was destined to be stripped and wounded by Life's wayside, while many passed him by unheeding."

The Christ at Emmaus is a small picture, and small the figures appear in that vast, dimly lighted chamber where the three are seated at table. The spiritual significance of Christ is suggested by most simple means. Light, and intensity of emotion, are the only aids. Rembrandt disdains all other effects. Intense feeling pervades the picture, even in the bare feet of Christ, even in the astonished hand of the disciple resting upon the chair; even in the back of the other disciple who gazes, with clasped hands, transfixed with amazement and love at the face of his Master, who has just broken bread and thus revealed Himself.

Of all Rembrandt's pictures, this was the one that made the profoundest impression upon the child when he had become a man. Other works, such as The Shipbuilder and his Wife at Buckingham Palace, The Syndics of the Drapers at Amsterdam, that ripe expression of Rembrandt's ripest powers, convinced him of the master's genius. He was deeply impressed by the range of portraits and subject-pictures at the Hermitage Gallery, many of which, by the art of Mr. Mortimer Menpes, have been brought to the fireside of the untravelled; but the Christ at Emmaus revealed to him the heart of Rembrandt, and showed him, once and for all, to what heights a painter may attain when intense feeling is allied with superb craftsmanship.

He found this intensity of emotion again in the Portrait of his Mother at Vienna. The light falls upon her battered, wrinkled face, the lips are parted as in extreme age, the hands, so magnificently painted, are folded upon her stick. When we look at Rembrandt's portrait of An Old Woman at the Hermitage Gallery, with that touch of red so artfully and fittingly peeping out from between the folds of her white scarf, we feel that he can say nothing more about old age, sad, quiescent, but not unhappy; when we look at the portrait of An Old Lady in the National Gallery (No. 1675) we feel that he can tell us no more about old age that still retains something that is petty and eager; but in the portrait of his mother at Vienna, Rembrandt, soaring, gives us quite another view of old age. It is the ancient face of a mother painted by a son who loved her, who had studied that face a thousand times, every

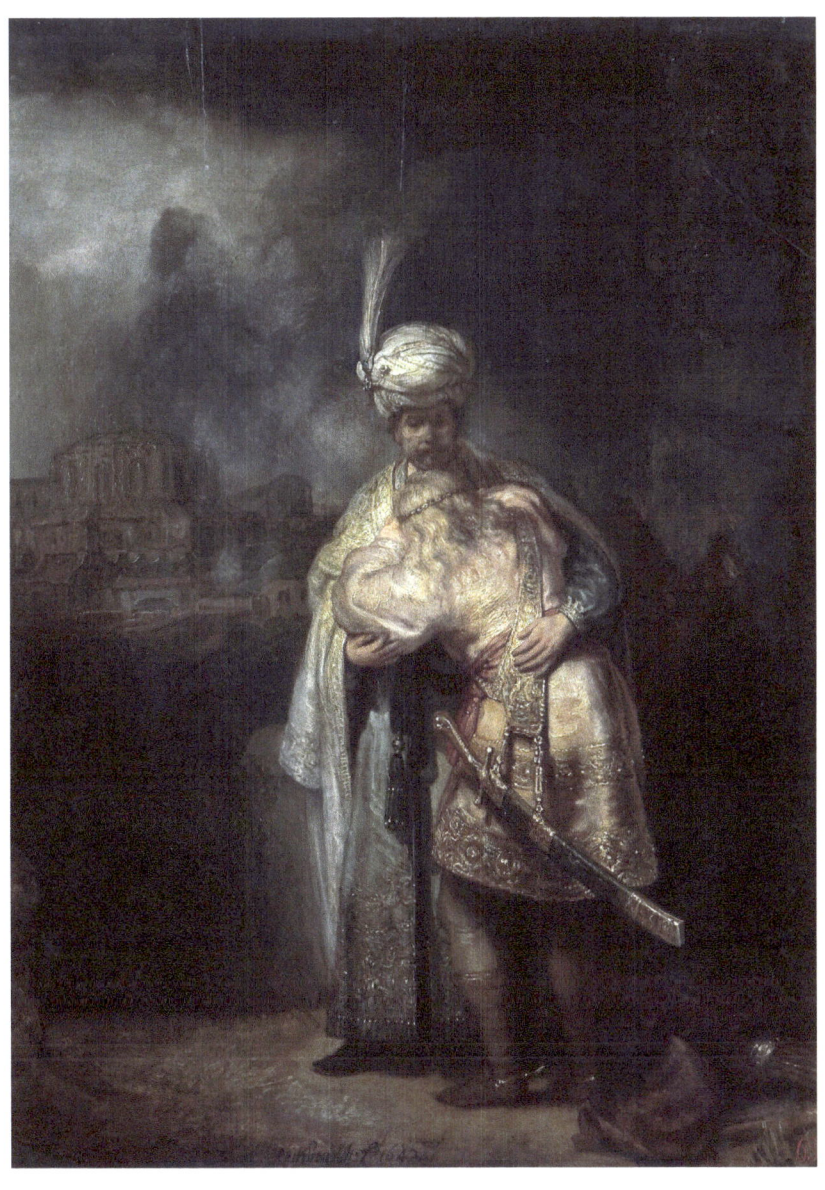

RECONCILIATION BETWEEN DAVID AND ABSALOM

1642. The Hermitage, St. Petersburg.

line, and light, and aspect of the features, and who stated all his love and knowledge upon a canvas.

Rembrandt was always inspired when he painted his own family. There is a quality about his portraits of father, mother, Saskia, Titus, and Hendrickje, yes! and of himself, that speaks to us as if we were intimates. It is a personal appeal. We find it in every presentment that Rembrandt gives us of another figure which constantly inspired his brush—the figure of Christ. In The Woman taken in Adultery, it is His figure that is articulate: it is the figure of Christ in the Emmaus picture that amazes: it is the figure of Christ that haunts us in a dozen of the etchings.

Slowly the child, now become a man, began, as he thought, to understand Rembrandt. Why did The Singing Boy at Vienna, apart from the quality of the painting, and the joy depicted on that young smiling face, make a personal appeal to him? Because he is Rembrandt's son, Titus; or if Titus was not actually the model, the features and the smile of Titus hovered between the father and the canvas.

He found an authentic portrait of Titus in the Wallace collection, painted in 1657, the year after Rembrandt had become bankrupt. It is one of the most charming portraits the master ever produced, a picture that even the most casual frequenter of galleries must pause before and love. A red cap crowns his curly hair, which falls to his shoulders. The face has a sweet expression; but the observant can detect traces of ill-health upon it. Titus died before his father. Father, mother, Saskia, Hendrickje, Titus, had all gone when the old man passed to his rest.

On the opposite wall at the Wallace collection is The Parable of the Unmerciful Servant, a fine example of Rembrandt the chiaroscurist, straightforward, but touched with that mystery so rare in painting, but which, under certain conditions, was as natural to Rembrandt as drawing. It is not always present in his work. None can say that there is any mystery

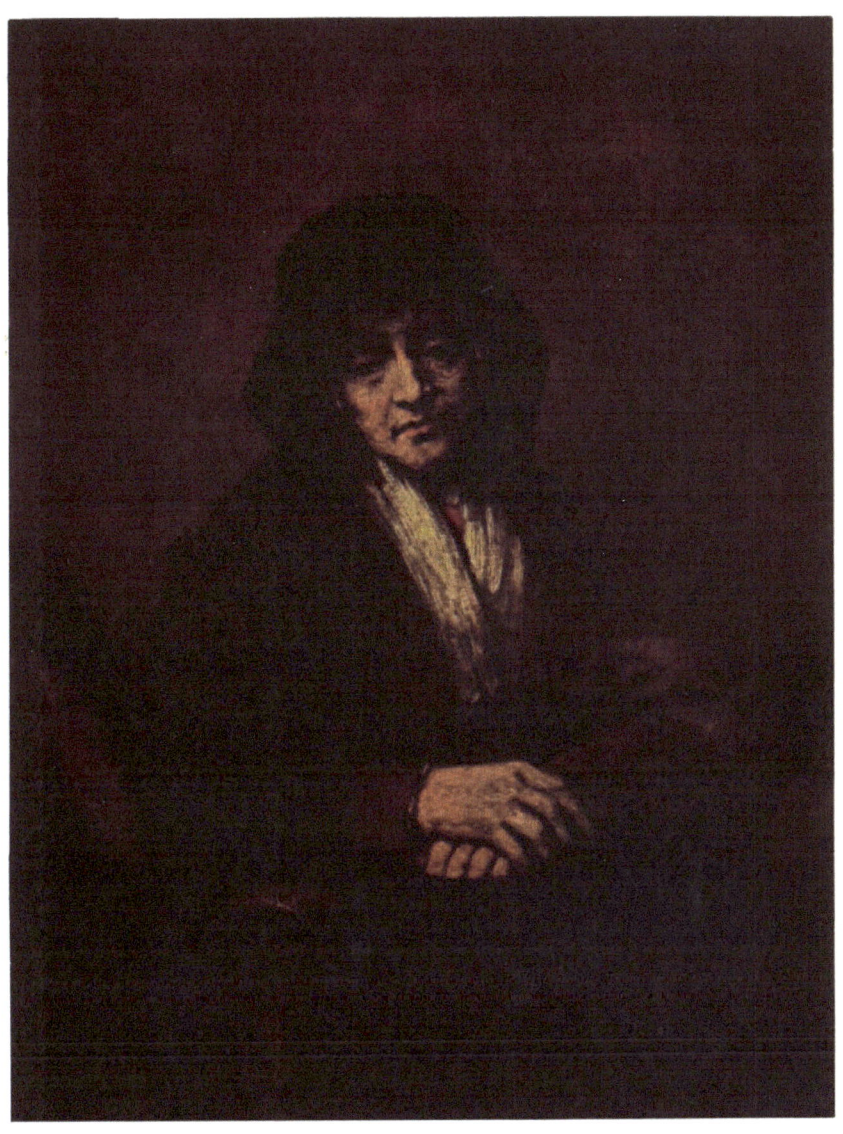

AN OLD WOMAN IN AN ARM CHAIR,

WITH A BLACK HEAD-CLOTH

1654. The Hermitage, St. Petersburg.

about the sober portrait pictures called The Wife of Jan Pellicorne with her Daughter, and Burgomaster Jan Pellicorne with his Son, in the Wallace collection. A scriptural subject was needed to inspire Rembrandt's brush with the sense of mystery.

It was the mystery of two pictures at the National Gallery that first drew the child to Rembrandt: it was the etchings that gave him a deeper insight into Rembrandt's sense of mystery, and made of him a willing Gamaliel at the master's feet.

CHAPTER III.

THE APPEAL OF THE ETCHINGS

The citizen and golfer, whose commerce with Rembrandt was narrated in the first chapter, approached the master through the writings of his Recoverers, certain art historians and scholars, who frequent libraries, search archives, and peruse documents; men to whom a picture is a scientific document rather than an emotional or intellectual experience. He was well content to end his commerce with Rembrandt there. History interested him: to art he was apathetic.

His son, as was indicated in the second chapter, was indifferent to art history, and he would not have walked across the road to read an unedited document; but I see him tramping ten miles to seek a picture that promised to stir his emotions and stimulate his imagination. Rembrandt, the maker of pictures, had become a vivid personality, a master whom he reverenced; but Rembrandt the etcher was unknown to him.

There are authorities who assert that in etching Rembrandt's art found its amplest and most exquisite expression. None will deny that his is the greatest name in etching. If all Rembrandt's pictures were destroyed, if every record of them by photograph or copy was blotted out, the etchings alone would form so ample a testimony to his genius that the name of Rembrandt would still remain among the foremost artists of the world.

Rembrandt enjoyed a period of popularity with his pictures, followed by years of decline and neglect, when lesser and more accommodating men ousted him from popular favour. But from first to last the products of his needle were appreciated by his contemporaries, even if he himself did not set great store by them. He began to etch early in life: he ceased only when his eyesight failed. He found in etching a congenial and natural means of self-expression. His artistic fecundity threw them off in regal profusion. The mood seized him: he would take a prepared plate, and sometimes, having swiftly spent his emotion, he did not trouble to do more than indicate the secondary incidents in a composition. Often he gave them away to friends and fellow-artists, or tossed them, when they had answered their purpose in his art life, so continuously experimental, into one of the sixty portfolios of leather recorded in the inventory of his property.

The history of Christ Healing the Sick, known as The Hundred Guilder Print, now the most prized of all the etchings, shows that he did not attach much value, either artistic or monetary, to this plate. He did not even receive a hundred guilders (under £9) for it, but gave the etching to his friend Jan Zoomer in exchange for The Pest, by M. Anthony. At the Holford sale, as has already been noted, £1750 was given for the Hundred Guilder Print.

It is supposed that only two of the etchings were made expressly for publication—the Descent from the Cross, and the Ecce Homo; but Rembrandt may have benefited from the sale of them through the partnership that was formed in 1660 between his son Titus and Hendrickje Stoffels.

In the eighteenth century certain connoisseurs had already made collections of his etchings. Catalogues began to be published, and in 1797 Adam Bartsch, keeper of the prints in the library at Vienna, issued the well-known catalogue that bears his name in two octavo volumes. Since

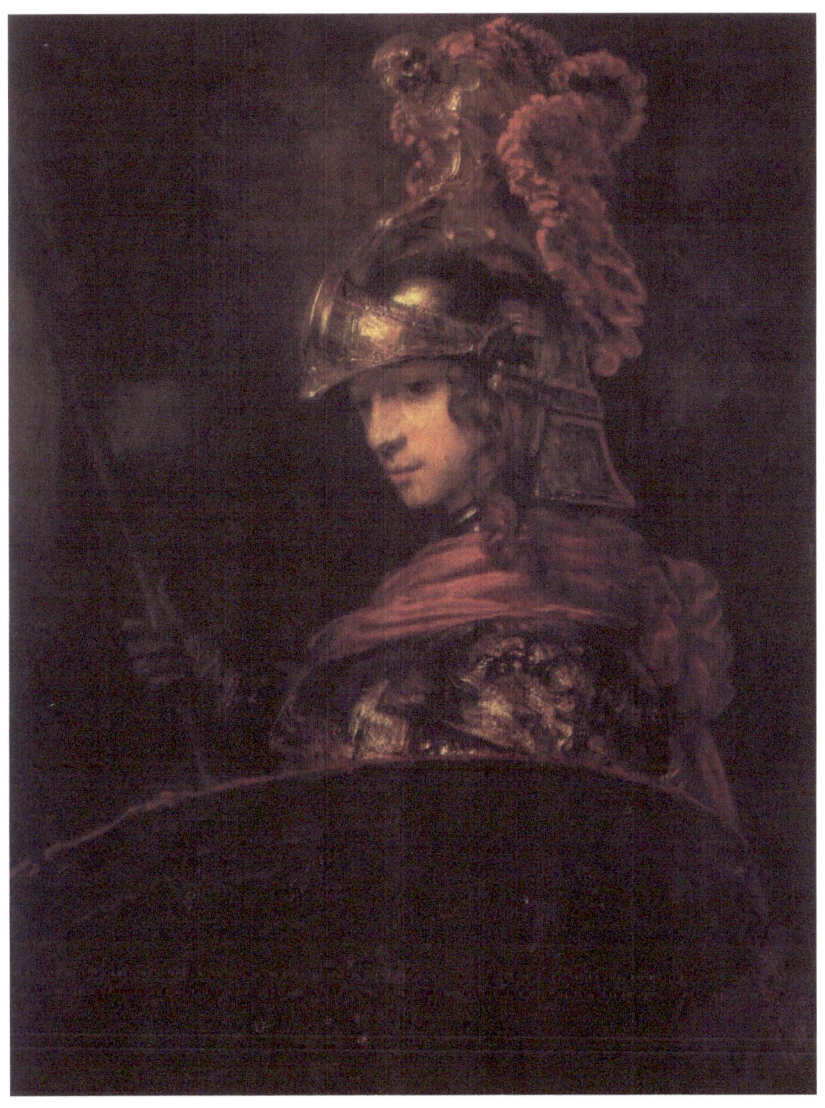

MINERVA

1655. The Hermitage, St. Petersburg.

Bartsch's monumental work many students of the etchings have striven to sift the authentic from the false. Needless to say, they disagree. Here are the figures:—

Bartsch	375	authentic etchings.
Wilson	366	" "
Claussin	365	" "
Blanc	353	" "
Middleton-Wake	329	" "
de Seidlitz	260	" "
Legros	71-113	" "

M. de Seidlitz's list of 260 was arrived at through consultation with several authorities, and that number is now accepted as approximately correct.

Our enthusiast knew nothing of the work of the labourers in Rembrandt's etching vineyard. He was quite ignorant of the expert contributions of Sir Francis Haden, P.G. Hamerton, and Mr. Frederick Wedmore, although his father, had he been a communicative man, could have discoursed learnedly on their efforts. Fate so willed it that he came to Rembrandt's etchings by chance, and, being sensitively alive to beauty and idealism, they merged into his life, and became as it were a personal possession.

On a certain day, in the window of one of those delightful London shops where first editions, prints, pieces of pottery, and odds and ends tempting to the virtuoso, are exposed for sale, he saw a small opulent picture by Monticelli. Entering to inquire the price, he discovered, as he had feared, that it was far beyond his bank balance. At the invitation of the proprietor, who seemed delighted that his goods should be admired, he stayed to "look round." Strewn upon a rosewood, inlaid table were a hundred and more etchings. Many were quite small, heads of men and women minutely and beautifully wrought; others, larger in size, were Biblical subjects; some were weird and fantastical; one, for example, showed a foreshortened figure lying before an erection, upon which a skinny bird stood with outstretched wings, flanked by ugly angel boys blowing trumpets.

"The best are sold," said the gentle proprietor.

The enthusiast was about to ask the name of the artist, when he suddenly caught sight of the Christ at Emmaus. His blood stirred in him. That little shop became an altar of art, and he an initiate. It was not the same version as the Louvre picture, but only one mind—the mind of Rembrandt, only one heart—the heart of Rembrandt, could have so felt and stated the pathos and emotion of that scene. Controlling his excitement, he turned over the prints and paused, startled, before Abraham's Sacrifice. What was it that moved him? He could hardly say. But he was moved to an extraordinary degree by that angel standing, with outstretched wings, by Abraham's side, hiding the kneeling boy's eyes with his hand, staying the knife at the supreme moment. He turned the prints, and paused again before The Prodigal Son. Some might call the face of the kneeling prodigal hideous, might assert that the landscape was slight and unfinished, that the figure in the doorway was too sketchy. Not so our enthusiast. This was the Prodigal Son, and as for the bending, forgiving father, all that he could imagine of forgiveness and pity was there realised in a few scratches of the needle. He turned the prints and withdrew Tobit Blind. In every line of this figure of the wandering old man, tapping his stick upon the pavement, feeling his way by the wall, was blindness, actual blindness—all the misery and loneliness and indignity of it.

"Are these for sale?" he asked the smiling proprietor, without the slightest hope that he could afford one.

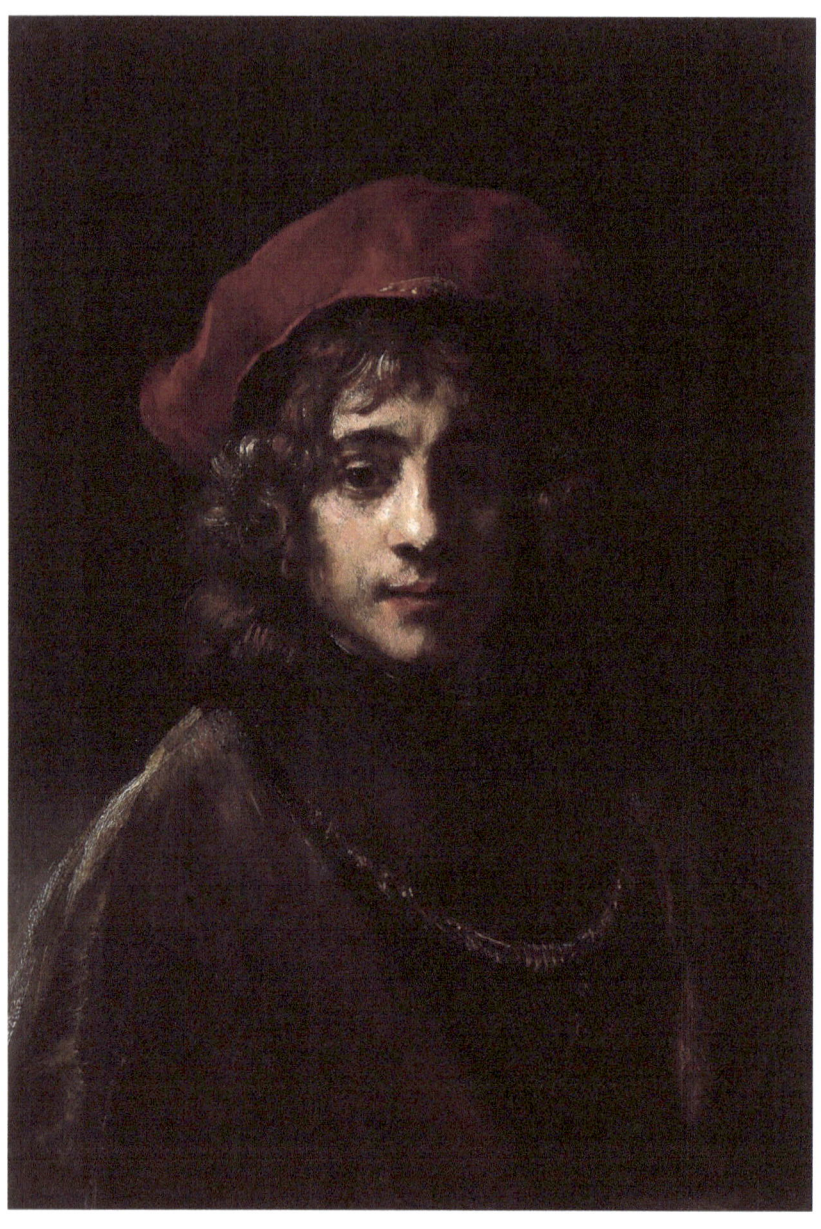

TITUS IN A RED CAP AND A GOLD CHAIN

1657. The Wallace Collection, London.

"Oh yes! Tobit Blind you can have for two shillings and sixpence. Abraham's Sacrifice, Christ at Emmaus, and The Prodigal Son are four shillings each."

The enthusiast could not conceal his astonishment. "I thought Rembrandt's etchings cost hundreds of pounds," he said.

"They do, but these are merely reproductions. Only a millionaire could hope to possess a complete collection of first states. These are the reproductions that were issued with M. Blanc's catalogue. He made them from the best proofs in his own collections, and from the public museums. You should compare them with the originals. The difference will astonish you. It's candle-light to sunlight, satinette to the finest silk."

"But where can I see the originals? I don't know any millionaires."

"Nothing easier! Go to the Print Room of the British Museum or to the Ionides Collection."

A day or two later the enthusiast, carrying under his arm the roll of four Rembrandt's etchings that he had purchased for fourteen shillings and sixpence, ascended the stairs of the British Museum, and timidly opened the door marked, "Print Room. Students only."

His reception agreeably surprised him. He, an obscure person, was treated as if he were a M. Michel. An obliging boy requested him to hang his hat and coat upon a peg, and to sign his name in a book. An obliging youth waved him to a noble desk running at a right angle to a noble window, and begged him to indicate his needs upon a slip of paper. He inscribed the printed form with the words—"Rembrandt's Etchings and Drawings."

The obliging youth scanned the document and said—"Which do you wish to see? There are many portfolios. I can bring you one at a time."

"Do so, if you please," said the enthusiast. "I should like to examine them all, even if it takes a week."

The obliging youth inclined his head and departed.

There is a delightful air of leisure and learning about the Print Room, and an entire absence of hustle. Two students besides himself were the only other members of the public, one studying Holbein, the other Blake.

The first portfolio that was brought to him contained the Christ Healing the Sick, known as The Hundred Guilder Print, in several states. It was the first large etching by Rembrandt that he had seen, and he gazed with astonishment, admiration, and awe at the almost miraculous characterisation of the figures, at the depth and richness of the blacks, and the nobility of the conception. He passed from that to The Three Crosses, and was even more moved by the dramatic intensity and realism of those burdened crosses against the profound gloom, and the dim, poignantly realised figures in the foreground. He saw the Christ before Pilate and The Death of the Virgin, lingering before them, studying every detail, realising to the full, through these splendid impressions, the height and significance of Rembrandt's genius. He compared the four prints he had purchased with their originals, and understood why collectors were eager to pay enormous prices for fine states, probably printed by the master himself.

As soon as he had finished one portfolio, the watchful attendant carried it away, and substituted another. It was so easy, so restful, and so invigorating to study a master under these conditions, that he wondered the public did not flock to the Print Room as to a first night at a popular theatre.

On another day he studied the drawings and landscape etchings—that dark, spacious design called The Three Trees, and a perfect little drawing of Joseph Consoling the Prisoners. The large plates inspired him with reverence and profound admiration for Rembrandt's genius as an etcher, but it was the smaller etchings that won his love and held

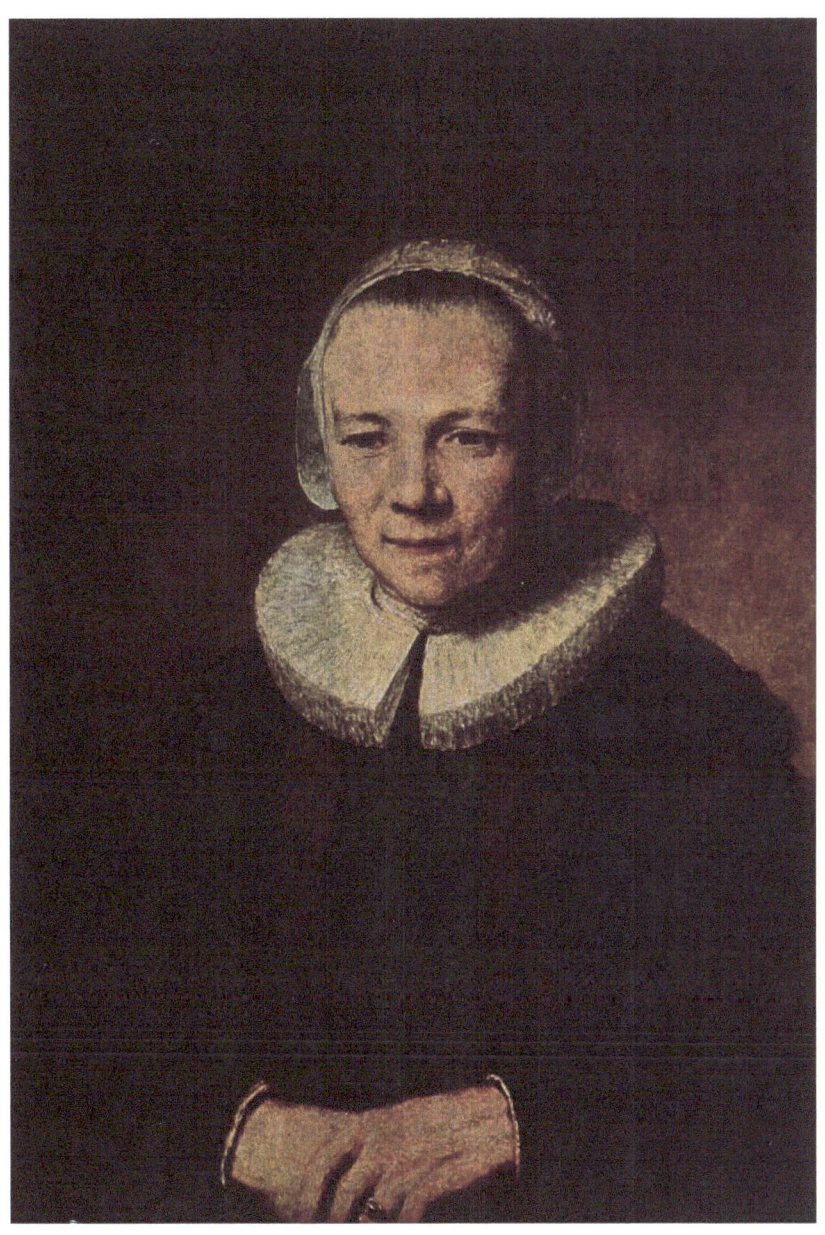

PORTRAIT OF AN OLD LADY, FULL

FACE, HER HANDS FOLDED

1641. The Hermitage, St. Petersburg.

it. He promised himself, when he came into certain family monies of which there was some prospect, that instead of buying an automobile, he would make himself the proud owner of The Three Trees, The Prodigal Son, Abraham's Sacrifice, and Tobit Blind—perhaps one, perhaps two, perhaps three, perhaps all four.

CHAPTER IV.

EPOCHS IN REM-
BRANDT'S LIFE

Suppose the admiration of our enthusiast for Rembrandt had been noted in the select suburb where he lived: suppose his mother was one of those estimable ladies who hold monthly Dorcas meetings in their drawing-rooms: suppose that while the ladies were working at useful garments for the poor, she persuaded her son to discourse on Rembrandt: suppose, because the petition came from his mother that he, very much against his will, consented.

It was not an easy task, as he took little or no interest in the life of Rembrandt; his interests were entirely with the æsthetic appeal of his work. What, he asked himself, can one say about the life of a man when that life was wholly one with his art—mingling with it, ministering to it at every point. A boy, the fifth child of a miller living at Leyden, is born into the world, takes to art as a duck to water, becomes one of the greatest painters of the world, dies in obscurity, is forgotten, and long after his death is placed among his peers. What is there to say about such a life? He made the attempt.

At the age of fourteen Rembrandt entered at Leyden University, but showed little inclination for books. He preferred Lucas van Leyden to Virgil, and his parents, accepting the situation, allowed him to study painting under Swanenburch, and later in the studio of Lastman at

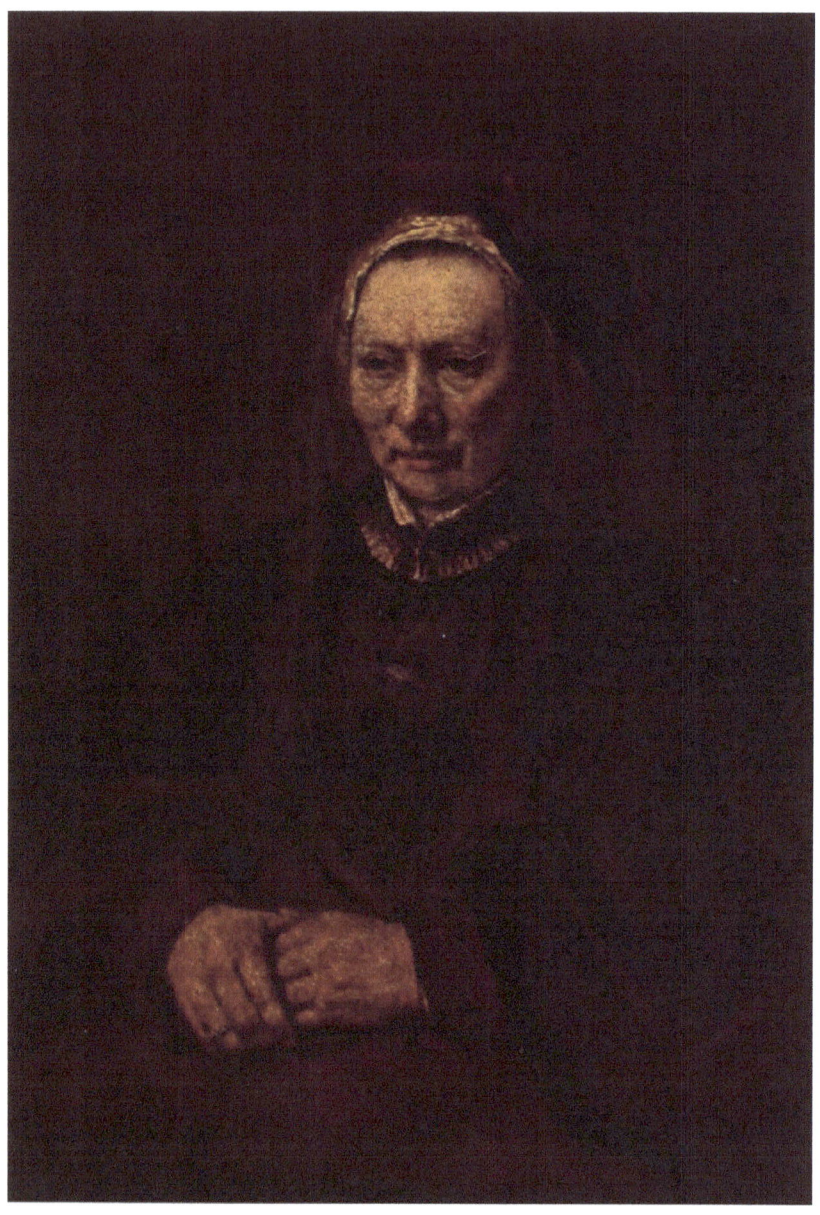

PORTRAIT OF AN OLD LADY IN A VELVET

HOOD, HER HANDS FOLDED

1650. The Hermitage, St. Petersburg.

Amsterdam. After a few months with Lastman he returned to Leyden, "to practise painting alone and in his own way." So much for his schooling. At the age of twenty-one he produced a picture called St. Paul in Prison, and Gerard Dou became his pupil. In 1631 he left Leyden and settled in Amsterdam. In 1634 he married Saskia van Uylenborch, who bore him three children, and Titus was the youngest. Some years later he had two daughters by his servant, Hendrickje Stoffels. Perhaps he married her. She was a kind, good soul, faithful and loyal to her master. His friends do not seem to have disapproved of this irregular union, but the Consistory of her church summoned Hendrickje before them and forbade her to communicate. At the age of fifty Rembrandt was declared bankrupt. From that date until his death troubles encompassed him; but he was happy so long as he could paint undisturbed. His son Titus died when he was sixty-two, and the following year Rembrandt died, and was buried at a cost of thirteen florins.

Our enthusiast did not find it easy to manipulate these facts, and he elected to slur over the Hendrickje episode; but he was able to interest the ladies of the Dorcas meeting by showing them some of Rembrandt's pictures. He collected a series of photographs of the portraits and paintings, including his favourite pictures, such as The Jewish Rabbi in the National Gallery, Titus and The Parable of the Unmerciful Servant in the Wallace collection, Rembrandt's Mother and The Singing Boy at Vienna; and he invested sixpence in a little manual recently published, called The Masterpieces of Rembrandt, containing sixty excellent reproductions of his portraits and pictures.

He also displayed photographs of the remarkable series in the Hermitage Gallery at St. Petersburg: The Descent from the Cross, with the brilliant light focussed on the body and winding sheet, and fading away into the darkness of the background; that radiant portrait of Saskia painted just before her marriage to Rembrandt, known as Flora with a Flower-trimmed Crook, standing at the opening of a grotto, with a wreath of flowers upon her head, and the light falling upon her face and gay attire; The Holy Family, the father working at his daily task in the background, and the Virgin, who has laid down her book, drawing aside the curtain from the cot to gaze upon the Child. He explained that Rembrandt, in placing this scene in a humble Dutch cottage, knew that he could express the Biblical story better that way than if he had painted an imaginary scene after the manner of the Italians.

"This great Dutch master" (he quoted from Mr. Colvin) "succeeded in making as wonderful pictures out of spiritual abjectness and physical gloom as the Italians out of spiritual exaltation and shadowless day."

At this point of his discourse he began to feel more confidence, and he proceeded to focus his remarks upon four periods in Rembrandt's life—epochs that lend themselves to separate treatment, each epoch marked by the production of a masterpiece, and one remarkable portrait that has a particular and pathetic interest. Those four pictures are The Anatomy Lesson, painted in 1632, when he was twenty-six; the Sortie of a Company of Amsterdam Musketeers, known as The Night Watch, painted in 1642, when he was thirty-six; The Syndics of the Cloth Hall, painted in 1662, when he was fifty-six; and his own portrait, painted in 1667, two years before his death. "His Anatomy Lesson," says M. Michel, "was the glorification of Science itself; in his Sortie of a Company of Amsterdam Musketeers he embodied that civic heroism which had lately compassed Dutch independence; and in a group of five cloth merchants seated round a table, discussing the affairs of their guild, he summed up, as it were, in a few immortal types, the noble sincerity of Dutch portraiture."

The Anatomy Lesson was the picture that gave Rembrandt his opportunity, and proclaimed his preeminence among the painters in

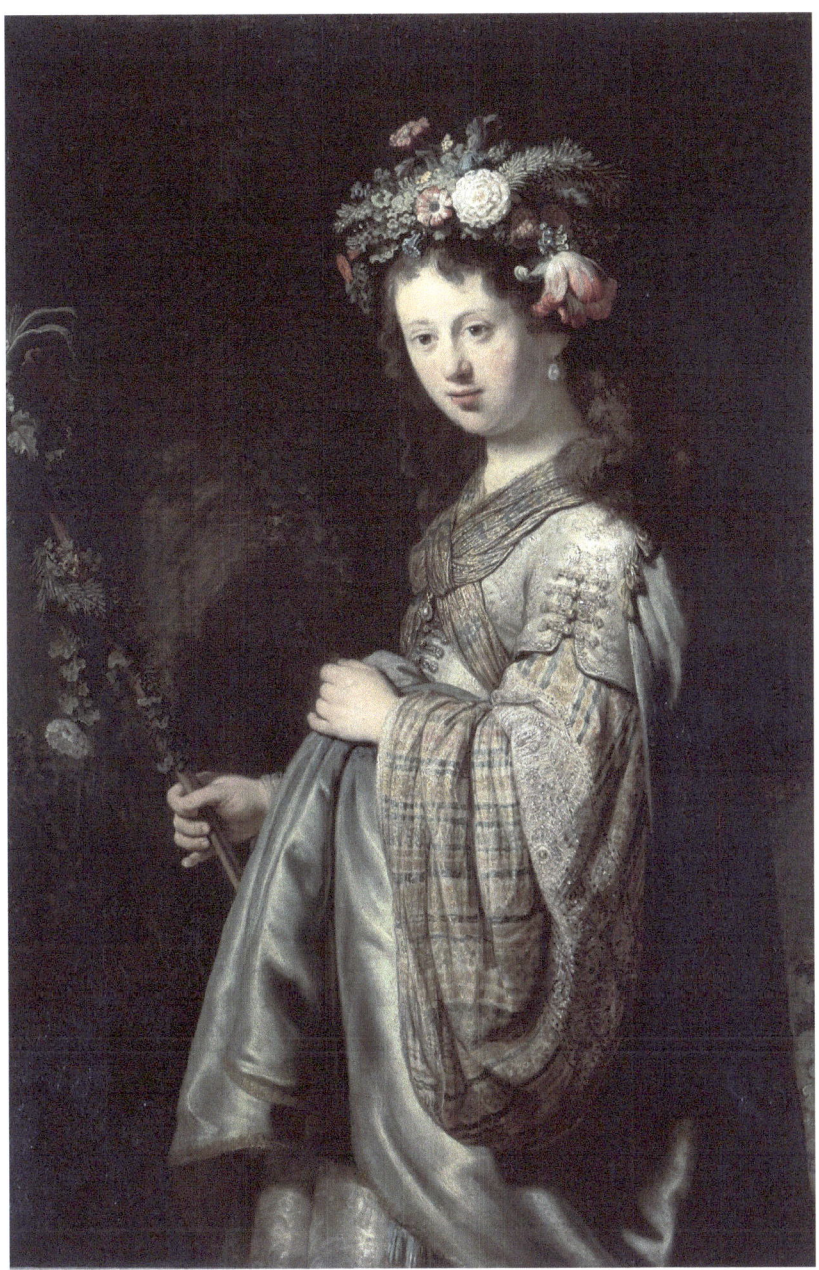

FLORA WITH A FLOWER-TRIMMED CROOK

1634. The Hermitage, St. Petersburg.

Amsterdam. It was the custom in those days for corporations, civic bodies, and associations of various kinds, to commemorate their period of office by commissioning portrait groups which should hand down their worthy faces to posterity. The desire of the less prominent members of the associations thus painted was that each head should be a likeness, plainly recognisable,—that one burgher should not be treated with more importance than another. This desire for present and posthumous commemoration extended to medical circles. Portraits and portrait groups of famous physicians and surgeons were painted and hung in the theatres where they lectured or operated. Dr. Tulp, an eminent surgeon of the day, commissioned Rembrandt to represent him performing an operation, proposing to present the picture to the Surgeons' Guild in memory of his professorship. The grave, realistic picture called The Anatomy Lesson, now hanging at the Hague Museum, was the result. The corpse lies upon the dissecting table; before it stands Dr. Tulp, wearing a broad-brimmed hat; around him are grouped seven elderly students. Some are absorbed by the operation, others gaze thoughtfully at the professor, or at the spectator. Dr. Tulp indicates with his forceps one of the tendons of the subject's left arm, and appears to be addressing the students, or practitioners, for these seven bearded men have long passed the age of studentship. This picture made Rembrandt's reputation. He was but twenty-six; the world seemed to be at his feet; in the two following years he painted forty portraits.

It was not easy for our enthusiast to explain to the ladies of the Dorcas meeting that the dissection of a body was a suitable subject for the brush of a painter. The Dutchmen of Rembrandt's day were not so squeamish as we have become since. They had a passion for the literal painting of literal things, and this picture was destined not for a Tate Gallery, but for the wall of an operating theatre. Dr. Tulp desired a picture of himself performing an operation, and Rembrandt gave it to him, painted in a way that pleased his contemporaries, and that has astonished the world ever since.

Ten years later Rembrandt painted another Doelen or Regent picture which, under the erroneous title of The Night Watch, is to-day the chief attraction of the Ryks Museum at Amsterdam. This time it was not a group of surgeons, but a company of Amsterdam musketeers marching out under the leadership of their captain, Frans Banning Cocq. In all these civic or military Regent pictures, each member subscribed a sum towards the artist's fee, and consequently each individual wished to have his money's worth in the shape of an accurate presentation of his face and form. It is an old quarrel between artist and public. Mr. Abbey had to face it in his Coronation picture; Mr. Bacon had to face it in his Return of the C.I.V.'s; perhaps the only folk who solved the problem were the complaisant gentlemen who designed panoramas of cricket matches in the last century, where each member of the company blandly faces the spectator. Much water had flowed under Burgomaster Six's bridge since Rembrandt painted The Anatomy Lesson. Then he was the obedient student. Now he was an acknowledged master. He painted The Sortie of the Company of Frans Banning Cocq as an artist who was profoundly interested in problems of light and shade, with strong views as to the composition of a picture, not as a methodical and mediocre painter desirous of carrying out the commission in a way to please his patrons. They wanted a presentment of the face and figure of each member of the company who had subscribed a hundred florins. Rembrandt gave them a work of art. No doubt the captain and his lieutenant were well enough pleased, for they stride forth in the forefront of the picture, but the rank and file were bitterly hostile. From the painting of The Night Watch his popularity began to wane.

The history of this picture, after it had been hung in the Doelen or assembly hall belonging to Captain Cocq's company, was as troublous as the later life of Rembrandt. Years afterwards when, blackened with smoke and ill-usage, it was removed from the Doelen to the Hotel de Ville, the authorities, finding that it was too large for the space it was destined to occupy, deliberately cut a piece away from each side. This is proved by a copy of the picture made by Lundens before the mutilation, now in the National Gallery. When M. Hopman undertook the restoration of The Night Watch he discovered, when he had removed the surface of dirt, that the sortie is taking place by daylight, and that the work contained something that Rembrandt evidently intended should represent a ray of sunlight. But the popular name of the picture is still The Night Watch.

The ladies of the Dorcas Society expressed in eyes and gestures their disapproval of the Amsterdam vandals who mutilated The Night Watch. One of them remarked: "It happened a long time ago. So gross a barbarity could not be perpetrated now."

Twenty years later, at the age of fifty-six, Rembrandt, having known what it was to be homeless and penniless, painted his masterpiece, The Syndics of the Cloth Hall, merely five figures grouped round a table, with a servant, uncovered, in attendance. It is an extraordinarily real picture, the final statement of Rembrandt's knowledge of painting, combined with that rare power of seeing things just as they are—the hundred subtleties that the untrained eye never sees, as well as the accents that all see. It is the perfect painter's vision—a scene grasped as a whole, character searched out but not insistent, the most delicate suggestion of equally diffused light knitting the figures together. He made no attempt to be picturesque as in The Night Watch; he was content just to paint five men dressed in black, with flat white collars and broad-brimmed hats, and a servant. With these simple materials

Rembrandt produced the picture that the world has agreed to regard as his masterpiece. Contemporary criticism says nothing about it. The place of honour at the Ryks Museum at Amsterdam is given to The Night Watch, but it is The Syndics of the Cloth Hall—a simple presentation of five grave men seated at a table—that we remember with wonder and admiration.

Our enthusiast, having dwelt upon these three masterpieces, marking epochs in Rembrandt's life, referred again to the magnificent array of portraits scattered in such regal profusion through the thirty years that passed between the painting of The Anatomy Lesson and The Syndics. Then noticing, while enlarging upon the etchings, that his mother was casting anxious glances at the clock, he hurriedly referred to the last portrait that Rembrandt painted of himself, two years before his death. He could not describe this portrait, which is in a private collection in Berlin, as he had never seen it, so he quoted M. Michel's description: "This extraordinary work, perhaps the last Rembrandt painted, is modelled with prodigious vigour and freedom. With superb audacity, the master shows us once more the familiar features, on which age and sorrow have worked their will. They are distorted, disfigured, almost unrecognisable. But the free spirit is still unbroken. The eyes that meet ours are still keen and piercing; they have even the old twinkle of good-humoured irony, and the toothless mouth relaxes in frank laughter. What was the secret of this gaiety? In spite of his poverty, he had still a corner in which to paint. Beside him stand an easel and an antique bust, perhaps a relic of his former wealth. He holds his maul-stick in his hand, and pauses for a moment in his work. He is happy because he can give himself up to his art."

It was the last of half a hundred portraits of himself, painted and etched without vanity; painted because a man's self is such an accom-

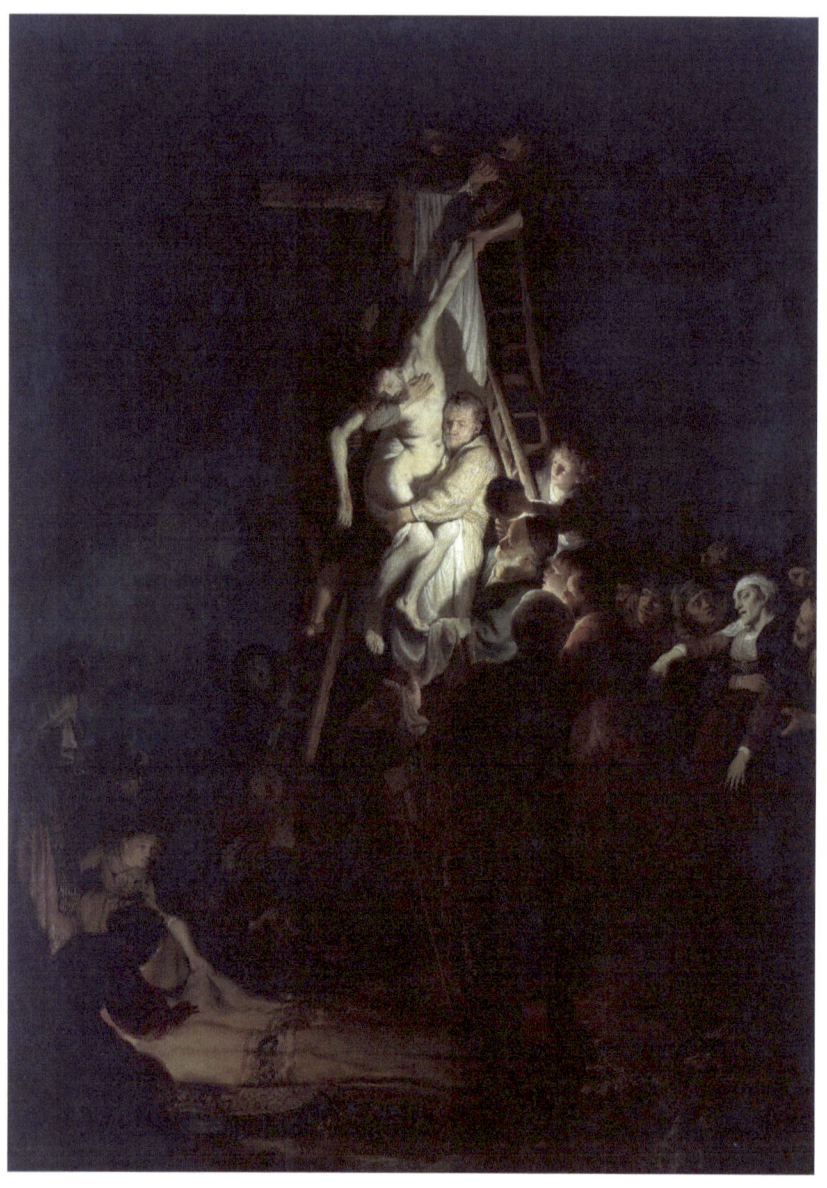

THE DESCENT FROM THE CROSS

1634. The Hermitage, St. Petersburg.

modating model, always ready and willing; painted because Rembrandt loved to experiment with himself before a mirror, grimacing, angry, stern, "as an officer," "with a casque," "with a gorget," or, as we see him in the National Gallery, on one wall with the bloom of youth and health upon his face, on the other, dulled, stained, and marked by the finger of time. This we can say: that he was always true to himself.

CHAPTER V.

THE GREAT TRIUMVIRATE

It is generally acknowledged that the greatest masters of painting that the world has known are Titian, Velasquez, and Rembrandt, and to each of the triumvirate we apply the word genius. Among the many definitions of that abused word is one which states that genius consists not in seeing more than other people, but in seeing differently. We acknowledge genius in a painter when, over and above masterly technical power, he presents to us a view of life or of nature which we may never have seen, but which we are convinced is the vision of deeper eyes than our own, and is true. The seer has seen it, and it is only because of the dimness or narrowness or worldliness of our outlook that we do not perceive it also.

A great painter writes us a letter, tells us of the things he has seen or heard or felt, gives us news of the world wherein he lives. He expresses his personality to us, and personality in art is a thing incalculable. Corot's Arcadia landscape delights us because it is the distilled essence of the vision, heart, and character of the personality called Corot. Personality may be expressed by a Rembrandt, abundantly. It may also be expressed by a Velasquez, negatively.

We must be vigilant, in judging a painter, to distinguish between his own personality and the personality of those who interpret him to us. The more we give of ourselves to a painter or an author, the greater is the return of his appeal and interest. Cleave the wood of your brain and you find him brimming with communications, raise the stone of your imagination and he is revealed.

A certain critic, who had devoted his life to the study of Reynolds, while lecturing upon the achievement of that master, threw upon the screen a certain large subject-picture, not one of Reynold's happiest efforts, but a laboured and unattractive design which, we know, gave Reynolds an infinity of trouble.

So scientific, so interesting was this critic's analysis of the picture, so absorbing the attributes he read into it, that many of his audience were persuaded that they were looking upon a Reynolds masterpiece, whereas they were but hypnotised by the subtleties of the critic's mind working upon Reynolds.

Conversely the criticism of some writers tends towards depreciation because of their predilection for objective as opposed to subjective criticism. The late P.G. Hamerton, writing upon Rembrandt, says, "The chiaroscuro of Rembrandt is often false and inconsistent, and in fact he relied largely on public ignorance. But though arbitrary, it is always conducive to his purpose."

"Conducive to his purpose!" There is much virtue in those four words. Rembrandt probably knew as well as anybody that his lighting of a picture was not a facsimile of the lighting of nature, or rather not the chiaroscuro as seen by the average eye; but he had an aim, a vision before him, and he did not hesitate to interpret that vision in his own way. Who dares to say that Rembrandt was disloyal to nature? Our concern is not what we should have done, but what Rembrandt did, seeing with his own eyes. And the questions we should ask ourselves are:—Is the interpretation of the world as seen through his eyes beautiful, suggestive, profound, and stimulating? Does the statement of his personality in paint add to our knowledge, educate our æsthetic perceptions, and extend our horizon by showing us things that our imperfect vision does not see except through him?

Comparisons are not only odious, but foolish. No sensible critic attempts a comparison between Titian, Velasquez, and Rembrandt. He accepts them as they are, and is grateful. But even the most obscure of mortals may have his preferences, and a curious chapter in the lives of individuals who have concerned themselves with painting would be the bewildering way in which the pendulum of their appreciation and admiration has swung backwards and forwards from Titian to Velasquez, from Velasquez to Rembrandt, and sometimes back to Titian. It is often a question of mood.

There are moods when the regal abundance, the consummate crafts-manship of Titian, the glow and splendour of his canvases, the range of them from The Man with the Glove in the Louvre to the Bacchus and Ariadne, force us to place him on the summit of Parnassus. We are dazzled by this prince of painters, dominating Venice at the height of her prosperity, inspired by her, having around him, day by day, the glorious pictures that the genius of Venice had produced. We follow his triumphant career, see him courted and fêted, recognise his detachment from the sorrow and suffering of the unfortunate and unclassed, and amid the splendour of his career note his avidity for the loaves and fishes of the world. Unlike Rembrandt, fortune favoured Titian to the end. His career was a triumphal progress. We stand in that small room at the Prado Museum at Madrid and gaze upon his canvases, sumptuous and opulent, diffusing colour like a sunset, indifferent to their story or meaning, happy and content with the flaming feast outspread for our enjoyment. We stand before his Entombment at the Louvre, dumb before its superlative painting, with hardly a thought for the tragedy that it represents. Titian accepts the lit-erary motive, and the artist in him straight forgets it. We walk from The Entombment to the little chamber where Rembrandt's Christ at Emmaus hangs, and the heart of Rembrandt is beating there. To Titian the glory of

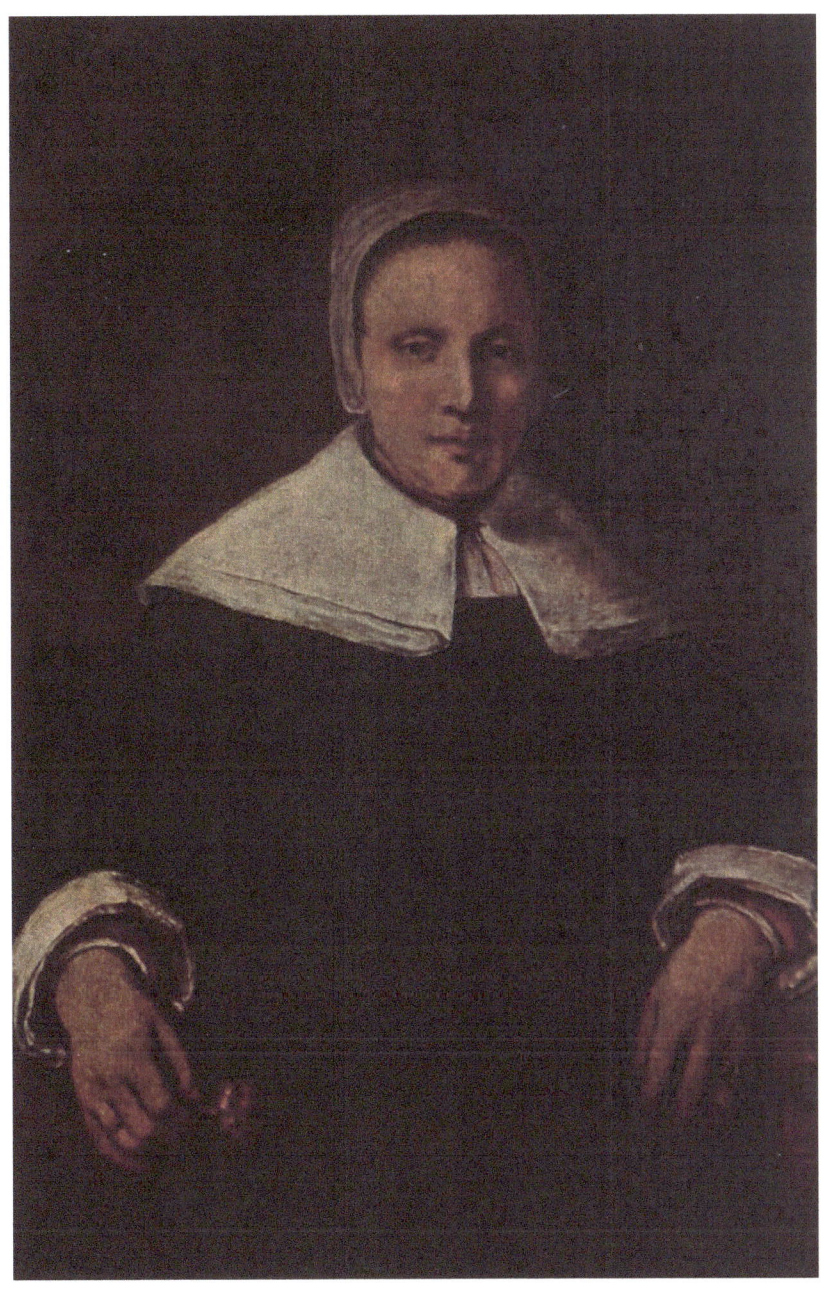

HER RIGHT HAND

1656. The Hermitage, St. Petersburg.

the world, to Rembrandt all that man has felt and suffered, parting and sorrow, and the awakening of joy. We do not compare the one painter with the other; we say: "This is Titian, that is Rembrandt; each gives us his emotion." Foolish indeed it seems in the face of these two pictures, and a thousand others, to say that art should be this or that,—that a picture should or should not have a literary or a philosophical motive. Painters give us themselves. We amuse ourselves by placing them in schools, by analysing their achievement, by scientific explanations of what they did just by instinct, as lambs gambol—and behind all stands the Sphinx called Personality.

There are moods when the appeal of Velasquez is irresistible. Grave and reticent, a craftsman miraculously equipped, detached, but not with the Jovian detachment of Titian, this Spanish gentleman stalks silently across the art stage. Hundreds of drawings of Rembrandt's exhibit evidence of the infinite extent of his experiments after perfection. The drawings of Velasquez can be counted on the fingers of one hand. He drew in paint upon the canvas. From his portraits and pictures we gather not the faintest idea of what he felt, what he thought, what he believed. One thing we know absolutely—that he saw as keenly and as searchingly as any painter who has ever lived. What he saw before him he could paint, and in the doing of it he was unrivalled. His hand followed and obeyed his eye. When the object was not before him, he falls short of his superlative standard. The figures of Philip IV., of Olivares, and of Prince Baltazar Carlos in the three great equestrian portraits are as finely drawn as man could make them. Velasquez saw them; he did not see the prancing horses which they ride, consequently our eyes dropping from the consummate figures are disappointed at the conventional attitudes of the steeds. Velasquez, like Titian, moved from success to success; both were friends of kings, both basked in royal favour, neither had the disadvantage, or perhaps the great advantage, like Rembrandt, of the education of adversity. Velasquez made two journeys into Italy; he knew what men had accomplished in painting, and if he was not largely influenced by Titian and Tintoretto, their work showed him what man had done, what man could do, and indicated to him his own dormant powers.

Rembrandt was sufficient unto himself. There are moods when one is sure that he stands at the head of the painting hierarchy. In spite of his greatness, we feel that he is very near to our comprehension. What a picture of the old painter towards the end of his life that saying of Baldinucci presents. We are told that near the close of his career, absorbed in his art, indifferent to the world, "when he was painting at his easel he had come to wipe his brushes on the hinder portions of his dress."

Rembrandt looms out like some amorphous boulder, stationary, lichen-stained, gathering time unto itself. He travelled so little that it can be said he was untravelled. The works of other painters affected him not at all. We are without proof that he was even interested in the work of his contemporaries or predecessors. Life was his passion. One model was as good as another. He looked at life, and life fired his imaginations. He painted himself fifty times; he painted his friends, his relations, and the people he met while prowling about the streets. His pencil was never idle. Imagination, which confuses the judgment of so many, aided him, for his imagination was not nourished by vanity, or the desire to produce an effect, but flowed from the greatness of his brooding heart. He stood alone during his life, an absorbed man, uninfluenced by any school; he stands alone to-day. The world about him, and his thoughts and reflections, were his only influences. He read few books, and the chief among them was the Bible. Mr. Berenson has written an exhaustive and learned work on Lorenzo Lotto, analysing his pictures year by year, and exhuming the various painters who influenced Lotto at the different periods of his life. Mr. Berenson's book extends to nearly three hundred pages. The influences of the painting fraternity upon Rembrandt would not provide material for the first paragraph of the first page of such a book.

His fame is assured. He is one of the great triumvirate. "He was greater, perhaps," says Mr. Clausen, "than any other painter in human feeling and sympathy, in dramatic sense and invention; and his imagination seemed inexhaustible."

The Ryks Museum at Amsterdam may be said to have been designed as a shrine for his Night Watch. Near by it hangs The Syndics of the Cloth Company, excelled, in this particular class of work, by no picture in the world; but it is by the portraits and the etchings that the sweep, profundity, and versatility of Rembrandt's genius is exemplified. Truly his imagination was inexhaustible.

It is an education to stand before his portraits in the National Gallery. Observe the Old Lady, aged 83, the massive painting of her face, and the outline of her figure set so firmly against the background. Here is Realism, frank and straightforward, almost defiant in its strength. Turn to the portrait of A Jewish Rabbi. Here is Idealism. You peer and peer, and from the brown background emerges a brown garment, relieved by the black cap, and the black cloak that falls over his left shoulder. Luminous black and luminous brown! Brown is the side of the face in shadow, brown is the brow in shadow. All is tributary to the glory of the golden brown on the lighted portion of the face. The portrait composes into a perfect whole. The dim blacks and browns lead up to the golden brown illuminating the old weary head, that wonderful golden brown—the secret of Rembrandt. This old Jew lives through the magic art of Rembrandt. He crouches in the frame, wistful and waiting, the eternal type, eternally dreaming the Jews' dream that is still a dream.

THE END